NEIGHBORHOOD HELPERS

Auto Mechanics

BY CECILIA MINDEN AND
MARY MINDEN-ZINS

The Child's World

Content Adviser:
Tony Molla, Vice President
of Communications, National
Institute for Automotive Service
Excellence, Leesburg, Virginia

Published in the United States of America by The Child's World®
PO Box 326
Chanhassen, MN 55317-0326
800-599-READ
www.childsworld.com

Acknowledgements

The Child's World®: Mary Berendes, Publishing Director

Editorial Directions, Inc.: E. Russell Primm, Editorial Director; Katie Marsico, Managing Editor and
Line Editor; Judith Shiffer, Assistant Editor; Caroline Wood, Editorial Assistant; Susan Hindman,
Copy Editor; Wendy Mead, Proofreader; Mike Helenthal, Rory Mabin, and Caroline Wood, Fact
Checkers; Tim Griffin/IndexServ, Indexer; Cian Loughlin O'Day, Photo Researcher; Linda S. Koutris,
Photo Selector

The Design Lab: Kathleen Petelinsek, Design and Art Production

Photographs ©: Cover: left, right/frontispiece—Stockdisc.
Interior: 4, 10, 17—Photodisc/Getty Images; 5—RubberBall Productions; 7—Jeff Kaufman/Taxi/Getty
Images; 8-9—Charles Gupton/Corbis; 11-left—SuperStock/Alamy Images; 11-right—Stockdisc; 12,
19—Mary Minden-Zins; 14-15—Juan Silva/The Image Bank/Getty Images; 20—David Beeler/Tran-
stock/Alamy Images; 22-23—Viennaphoto/allOver photography; 24—David Madison/The Image
Bank/Getty Images; 26-27—Ken Kaminesky/Take 2 Productions/Corbis; 28-29—Ariel Skelley.

Library of Congress Cataloging-in-Publication Data

Minden, Cecilia.
  Auto mechanics / by Cecilia Minden and Mary Minden-Zins.
    p. cm. — (Neighborhood helpers)
  ISBN 1-59296-560-1 (library bound : alk. paper)
1. Automobiles—Maintenance and repair—Vocational guidance—Juvenile literature. 2. Automobile
mechanics—Juvenile literature. I. Minden-Zins, Mary. II. Title. III. Series.
  TL152.M4452 2006
  629.28'72023—dc22
                                        2005026010

TABLE OF CONTENTS

Hello. My name is Javier. Many people live and work in my neighborhood. Each of them helps the neighborhood in different ways.

I thought of all the things I like to do. I like using my hands. I like to figure out how things work. I like looking at different cars.

How could I help my neighborhood when I grow up?

The American Motor Company opened a repair garage in New York in 1899. Repair garages soon opened in other large cities. Repair garages were all over the United States by the mid-1950s.

I COULD BE AN AUTO MECHANIC!

Auto mechanics are very good at figuring out how things work. They know how to use their hands to fix things.

Best of all, auto mechanics get to be around all kinds of cars!

Kids who like cars and enjoy fixing things might make good auto mechanics.

LEARN ABOUT THIS NEIGHBORHOOD HELPER!

The best way to learn is to ask questions. Words such as *who, what, where, when,* and *why* will help me learn about being an auto mechanic.

Asking an auto mechanic questions is a good way to learn more about his job.

Where Can I Learn More?

Automotive Service
Association
PO Box 929
Bedford, TX 76095

National Institute for
Automotive Service
Excellence (ASE)
101 Blue Seal Drive SE
Leesburg, VA 20175

How Can I Explore This Job?

Does a parent or other adult you know work on cars? Ask if you can watch or maybe help. Work on fixing your own bicycle. You'll become familiar with some of the tools mechanics use.

WHO CAN BECOME AN AUTO MECHANIC?

Boys and girls who want to know about cars and how they work may want to become auto mechanics. People who want to be auto mechanics also need to know how the different parts in a machine all work together. Auto mechanics are very important to the neighborhood.

They make sure people's cars are working the right way. It would be hard for people to get to work and school if they didn't have working cars.

Auto mechanics make sure that people in the neighborhood have working cars.

MEET AN AUTO MECHANIC!

This is John Ahooei. John is an auto mechanic in Oklahoma City, Oklahoma. When John is not at his shop, he likes to spend time with his family. He also loves to play soccer, and he coaches a children's soccer team.

John Ahooei works as an auto mechanic in Oklahoma.

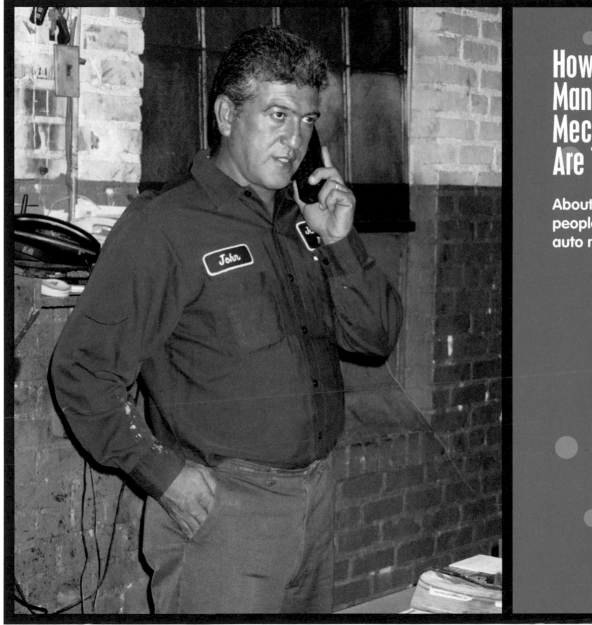

How Many Auto Mechanics Are There?

About 818,000 people work as auto mechanics.

WHERE CAN I LEARN TO BE AN AUTO MECHANIC?

John went to the University of Oklahoma, but people don't have to go to college to become auto mechanics. They can work with people who are already auto mechanics and learn how to fix different cars. They can also go to **vocational schools** that offer classes for auto mechanics.

John stills takes classes to learn new and better ways of working on cars. He wants to be sure his customers get the best service.

Students get hands-on training at vocational schools. They work with tools they will one day use as auto mechanics.

How Much School Will I Need?

Most auto mechanics have high school diplomas. Many mechanics have taken more classes at vocational schools and passed tests. These mechanics are then given certification. Someone who gets certification proves they have the abilities to work in a certain profession.

vocational schools (voh-KAY-shun-ul SKOOHLZ) special schools where people learn skills needed for different trades

What Are Some Tools I Will Use?

Computerized testing machines

Hand tools

Power tools

socket and ratchet set (SOK-iht AND RA-chit SEHT) a tool set used to tighten and loosen different car parts

WHAT DOES AN AUTO MECHANIC NEED TO DO HIS JOB?

A car has many parts that must all work together to make it run safely. An auto mechanic has to know the name of each part and which tools can be used to repair it.

One set of tools John uses is called a **socket and ratchet set.** John's tools must be very strong so they do not break when he is working on heavy machinery.

A very important car part is the car battery. Do you have a toy car that uses a battery? A car battery is much larger because it needs to give a real car more power. John has to know how to take out an old battery and put in a new one.

What Clothes Will I Wear?

Goggles

Earplugs

Work shirts and pants or uniform

Work shoes or boots

What Is It Like Where I'll Work?

Garages are usually clean and well-lighted. Sometimes they are noisy because of power tools and engines. Mechanics often work in tight, cramped spaces for a long time.

WHERE DOES AN AUTO MECHANIC WORK?

John has owned John's Auto Shoppe for fifteen years. It is a small business with four auto mechanics. John teaches his workers to treat each car as if it were their own.

John's day begins when a customer brings in a car for repair. John has to figure out what's wrong with the car. He spends time talking to the car's owner.

Four mechanics work at John's Auto Shoppe in Oklahoma City.

John also asks if the car is making any odd sounds.

John tries to figure out what is wrong with the car. He may call an auto parts store so he can get a new part to replace the old one.

John then goes to work on the car. After the car is fixed, he takes it for a **test drive.** John returns the car to the customer if the test drive goes well.

Auto mechanics sometimes use computers to figure out what is wrong with a car.

How Much Money Will I Make?

Most auto mechanics make between $22,000 and $41,000 a year.

test drive (TEHST DRIYV) when a mechanic drives a car to make sure everything works

What Other Jobs Might I Like?

Aircraft mechanic

Automobile collision repairer

Bus and truck mechanic

Motorcycle mechanic

WHO WORKS WITH AUTO MECHANICS?

John fixes many cars, but sometimes other people help his customers, too. Workers at a body shop often repair dents and other damages caused by accidents. John also knows people who do the detailing on cars. They help cars stay in good shape by carefully cleaning them inside and out.

Workers at a body shop often help repair cars that are dented or damaged.

WHEN DOES AN AUTO MECHANIC GET TO WORK ON A RACE CAR?

Some auto mechanics are specially trained to take care of race cars. It is important for auto mechanics who work on these cars to know a lot about them. Race cars often need special parts. Auto mechanics have to know how to fix all of these parts. Wouldn't it be fun to take a race car for a test drive?

Vrooom! Some auto mechanics are responsible for taking care of race cars.

How Might My Job Change?

Mechanics may eventually work with specific systems or parts of a car. Other mechanics may open their own businesses.

I WANT TO BE AN AUTO MECHANIC!

I think being an auto mechanic would be a great way to be a neighborhood helper. Someday I may be the person fixing your car!

Who's working on that car?
One day it may be you!

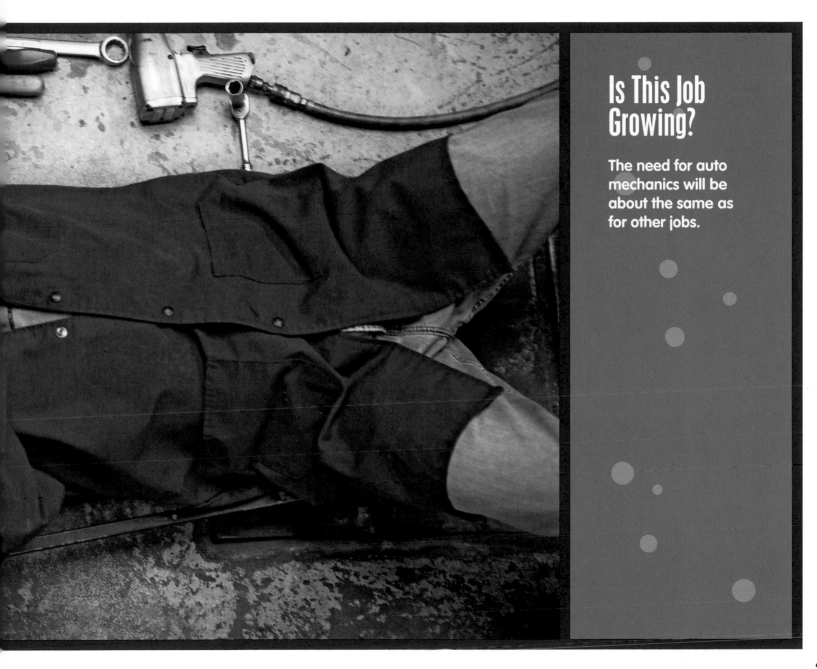

Is This Job Growing?

The need for auto mechanics will be about the same as for other jobs.

WHY DON'T YOU TRY BEING AN AUTO MECHANIC?

Do you think you would like to be an auto mechanic? You can get practice by learning how to take care of your bike. Ask an adult to help you make sure your bike is safe to ride:

- Check the bike seat, handlebars, and wheels. They should fit snugly.
- Check the chain. It should be oiled and move smoothly.
- Check the brakes. They should work well and not stick.
- Check the tires. They should have enough air.

Caring for your bike is a good way to practice being an auto mechanic.

I Didn't Know That!

There are more than 200 million cars in the United States!

HOW TO LEARN MORE ABOUT AUTO MECHANICS

BOOKS

Flanagan, Alice K., and Romie Flanagan (photographer). *Mr. Yee Fixes Cars.* Danbury, Conn.: Children's Press, 1998.

Florian, Douglas. *An Auto Mechanic.* New York: Greenwillow Books, 1991.

Korman, Justine, and Steven James Petruccio. *At the Auto Repair Center.* New York: Scholastic, 1999.

Weintraub, Aileen. *Auto Mechanic.* Danbury, Conn.: Children's Press, 2003.

WEB SITES

Visit our home page for lots of links about
auto mechanics:
http://www.childsworld.com/links

Note to Parents, Teachers, and Librarians:

We routinely check our Web links to make sure they're
safe, active sites—so encourage your readers to check
them out!

ABOUT THE AUTHORS:

Dr. Cecilia Minden is a university professor and reading specialist with classroom and administrative experience in grades K–12. She is the author of many books for early readers. Cecilia and her husband Dave Cupp live in North Carolina. She earned her PhD in reading education from the University of Virginia.

Mary Minden-Zins is an experienced classroom teacher. She taught first-grade for ten years before taking time out to raise her five children and play with her four grandchildren. Mary now teaches kindergarten and lives in Oklahoma with her dog, Nick; her turtle, Herman; and her grandson's two cats, Mitten and Jessica.

INDEX